Totally Amazing
Careers in
ENGINEERING

Sally Ride
Science

CONTENTS

Susan

Jan

Oksana

Oren

Natalie

Alexandria

Chuck

Angela

Krishna

Ayanna

Emir

Mark

What Do You Want To Be?

It's never too soon to think about what you want to be.

You probably have lots of things you like to do—maybe you like doing experiments or drawing pictures. Or maybe you like working with numbers or writing stories.

Is being an engineer one of your goals? The good news is that there are many different paths leading there. The people in engineering come from many different professions—from chemists, environmentalists, inventors, to programmers, doctors, and more.

SALLY RIDE
First American Woman in Space

The women and men you're about to meet found their careers by doing what they love. As you read this book and do the activities, think about what you like doing. And follow your interests. You just might find your career, too.

Reach for the stars!

Sally K Ride

SUSAN HELMS
United States Air Force

Flying High

Susan Helms wanted to join the Air Force from the time she was little, but she didn't have good enough eyesight to be a pilot. Next choice? Aerospace engineering! While working on the missiles that are attached to fighter jets, she thought, "There must be a way that an engineer can start flying." Well, there was. Susan trained as a flight test engineer and designed tests to study the way airplanes work in the sky. Then she got to sit behind the pilot—in more than 30 types of military aircraft—as he or she ran those tests and pushed the machines to their limits, screaming across the sky. "I don't remember the scary moments," Susan tells Sally Ride Science. "I just remember the thrill of having a good time and doing a good job at the same time."

Above and Beyond

Then Susan really took off—into orbit. She became an astronaut and flew on four space shuttle missions. The highlight of her career came in 2001, when she lived on the International Space Station for six months as part of its second crew.

Susan set the record for the longest space walk ever—nearly nine hours!

An aerospace engineer

works on technology for air or space travel. Susan tested planes, then became an astronaut. Other **aerospace engineers**

* build rockets, satellites, and Mars landers.

* test vehicle parts in wind tunnels.

* model airplanes in 3-D on computers.

* develop new airplane or rocket engines.

Going Up?

If you could live in a space station, how long would you want to stay? What would you take with you?

_____

_____

_____

_____

Be a Flight Test Engineer

Compete with your friends to see who can design the paper airplane that can go the farthest or stay in the air the longest.

What was different about the plane that flew the farthest? _____

_____

What was different about the plane that stayed in the air the longest? _____

_____

Your Turn

"I was creative as a kid and took a lot of art lessons," Susan says. "The neat thing about engineering is that it's kind of the ultimate combination between mathematics and creativity." In graduate school, Susan got to sketch airplane designs. Grab some paper and try out your own creativity by sketching whatever you'd like.

"When you have a passion for something, you don't listen to people who say you can't."

JAN TALBOT
University of California, San Diego

Always a Challenge

In college, Jan Talbot was in classes with hundreds of other students—and sometimes she was the only woman. When the professor would say, "Good morning, gentlemen," she had to wave her hand to remind him she was there, too! She says she never got discouraged. Jan decided to focus on chemistry because it was her worst subject. That way, Jan laughs, she would always have a good challenge to enjoy.

Variety Is the Spice of Life

Jan combines chemistry, physics, math, and engineering in her work. "I like the variety and the ability to use all those tools to solve a problem," she says. Jan does lots of experiments. She uses chemistry to create better materials, including ones used to make the flat-panel screens that are popular in today's computers and televisions. Another growing field is nanotechnology—making incredibly small things atom by atom or molecule by molecule.

Jan enjoys a challenge such as a hike in the desert.

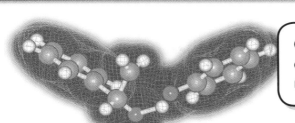

Chemists can build and experiment with models of molecules on a computer.

Chemical Recipes

Chemists use chemical "formulas" to describe the elements, or basic ingredients, that form compounds.

Can you match the chemical formulas to the compounds listed below?

A chemical engineer uses chemistry to find new, different, and better ways to do lots of things that affect the way we live, including

* producing gasoline from oil.
* cleaning up polluted drinking water.
* developing flavors for foods and drinks.
* creating fireproof fabrics.
* inventing environmentally friendly paints.

$C_{12}H_{22}O_{11}$ Baking Soda

H_2O Sugar

$NaCl$ Salt

CO_2 Water

$NaHCO_3$ Carbon Dioxide

Here's What U Think

Some products in my house that might have been created by chemical engineers are _____

Some things I'd like to invent are _____

I think about the way things taste, smell, feel or look. The sense I react to most strongly is _____ because _____
_____

Something that I use every day but think could be improved is _____

It could be improved by _____

Want to check your answers? Check 'Em Out on page 32.

"We get to enjoy the attractions ourselves, and we get to see our guests enjoy them too."

OKSANA WALL

Walt Disney World

Dreams Really Do Come True

When Oksana Wall was 13, she and her family came from Venezuela to visit Walt Disney World®. She wondered who created the rides. When she found out they were designed by engineers, she decided that was what she would become. For Disney. Eventually her dream came true. Now she works on all kinds of rides, making sure they're fun, safe, and unique. "I really love getting to work on such a great variety of projects," Oksana says. "I have a blast at my job."

Make-Believe Is True Fun

Oksana gets to work with electrical engineers, mechanical engineers, structural engineers, industrial engineers, architects, and the people who dream up the rides in the first place. "What makes a good ride is to have a great marriage of technology and creativity that truly takes the guest into a make-believe world," she says.

Imagineering

What's it like to fly? Or to be a rock star? Or to make friends with a cartoon character? Is it the job of an engineer to answer these questions? Yes—if she works at Walt Disney World® Resort.

A civil engineer designs

and manages structures that lots of people use. Oksana designs amusement park rides. Other **civil engineers**

* manage the construction of skyscrapers and stadiums.

* plan highways, railways, and airports.

* design large structures such as bridges or dams.

* purify wastewater and industrial waste.

What Would U Do?

If you could design an amusement park ride, what would it be like? If you want, sketch it out on paper.

_____

_____

_____

_____

Civil Projects

Across

5. The tunnel under the English Channel connecting England to France.

7. Engineers created an entire _____off the coast of Japan just so an airport could be built on it.

Down

1. The world's tallest _____ is in Taiwan and has 101 floors.

2. When demolishing a building, engineers use explosives to make it fall inwards, or _____.

3. Ancient Romans used _____ to bring water to cities.

4. Sitting at the top of a rollercoaster, a train has a lot of potential energy. Coming down, it has _____ energy.

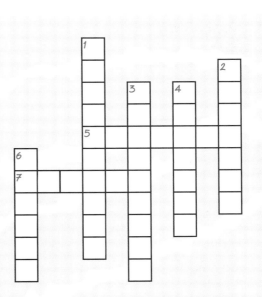

6. The largest civil engineering project in US history required building two tunnels and a bridge in Boston. It's called The _____ _____.

Want to check your answers? Check 'Em Out on page 32.

11

OREN JACOB
Pixar Animation Studios

Movies Move

Imagine making movies on computers, and getting paid for it. Welcome to Oren Jacob's job as a computer graphics engineer at Pixar Animation Studios. He's been technical director on computer-animated films, such as *Finding Nemo* and *Toy Story 2*—overseeing the other engineers and hi-tech methods used to animate all the creatures and their surroundings. For example, each pelican in *Finding Nemo* had about 50,000 individual feathers—each feather was created on a computer, and each was programmed to move separately!

Making H_2O Flow

Oren started as an intern at Pixar Animation Studios when he was studying mechanical engineering in college. "I studied how fluids move," Oren tells Sally Ride Science. "Good thing, too, because we had to simulate the way water flows and splashes in almost every single shot in *Finding Nemo*."

Hot Dog!

In elementary school, Oren started learning about and loving computers. He also loved movies. His mother used to take Oren and his friends to the movies and then talk about them over hot dogs and cookies. Let's see: computers and movies—sounds like the rest is movie history.

> **Behind Oren is a blowup of a sea anemone drawn by one of the designers of *Finding Nemo*.**

A computer graphics engineer

A computer graphics engineer uses computers to create animated characters and scenery, and then make the characters move and interact with each other. Oren oversees the graphics for animated movies. Other **computer graphics engineers**

* produce visual effects for live–action movies such as *Lord of the Rings.*

* design and create video games.

* create and animate special effects or mini-movies for Web sites.

Write and Draw

If you could work on an animated movie, what would the story be about? Who would the characters be? Now sketch the main character of the movie.

Did U Know?

For one scene where Nemo is riding with the turtles, engineers at Pixar had to simulate five miles of an ocean current, create 300,000 individual bubbles, and draw a million tiny bits of matter in the water to make things look real.

Movie Homework

Oren suggests that in order to learn about computer animation, it's best to study animated movies. Watch a movie on DVD or video, such as *Finding Nemo*, and pause the movie every few minutes. Try this several times. What do you see?

SCENE	LIGHTING	CHARACTERS' EXPRESSIONS	BACKGROUND DESCRIPTION

NATALIE JEREMIJENKO
University of California at San Diego

Go Fetch

If you see a pack of robotic dogs sniffing a landfill near your home, don't be alarmed. Natalie Jeremijenko and her students are probably there. She likes to buy cheap robotic toy dogs and take them apart. Her students install new brains, new legs, and new noses so e-Fido and pals can trek off-road to search for nasty toxins. Polluters, beware of dog.

Science That's Hard to Miss

Natalie's done lots of cool tech designs: a toy spy plane, a kid's pony ride that shakes to recreate a big 1989 earthquake, some remote-controlled geese, and a program that prints a slice of tree whenever your printer uses a tree's worth of paper. She's famous for dozens of cloned trees that she planted around San Francisco to illustrate environmental effects on growth. The common thread: all her projects present scientific ideas and data in ways that grab your attention.

Crossing Boundaries

So is Natalie an artist or an engineer? Well, in school she jumped between neuroscience, computers, art, and mechanics. "You can ask the same questions from different points of view as a way to develop a better understanding," she tells Sally Ride Science. "It doesn't feel like I'm jumping around at all."

A design engineer can come from different engineering backgrounds, but must be creative. Natalie builds things that present information in new ways. Other **design engineers**

* write multimedia software.
* design sleek new vehicles.
* create cool electronic devices such as iPods.
* build homes that look cool and save energy.

Your Pet Bot

If you could program a robotic dog to go anywhere and do anything, what would you have it do?

_____

_____

_____

Is Design Engineering 4 U?

What parts of Natalie's job would you like?

❑ Building machines

❑ Helping people learn about science

❑ Making products more useful

❑ Writing about how technology changes our lives

Feature Finder

When brainstorming and developing a new product, design engineers often think about these features.

AERODYNAMIC	PORTABLE
CHEAP	RECYCLABLE
EASY TO FIX	RECYCLED
EASY TO USE	STRONG
ERGONOMIC	STYLISH
MARKETABLE	UNIQUE

```
A  K  E  R  G  O  N  O  M  I  C
K  E  O  X  Q  M  K  J  A  D  P
C  I  M  A  N  Y  D  O  R  E  A
K  X  F  I  E  M  K  N  K  L  E
E  S  U  O  T  Y  S  A  E  C  H
E  L  B  A  T  R  O  P  T  Y  C
R  H  S  I  L  Y  T  S  A  C  D
I  G  N  O  R  T  S  O  B  E  H
D  U  N  I  Q  U  E  A  L  R  Y
E  L  B  A  L  C  Y  C  E  R  E
```

Want to check your answers? Check 'Em Out on page 32.

ENVIRONMENTAL ENGINEER

ALEXANDRIA BOEHM

Stanford University

"That's definitely what I enjoy most—being outside doing science."

Environmental engineers develop alternative sources of energy, such as wind turbines.

Diving In

Ali Boehm is never far from water—whether working or playing. Growing up in Hawaii, she loved to snorkel, scuba dive, and surf. When the places where she swam started filling with pollution, she knew something had to be done. "I've been an environmentalist since I was really young," she tells Sally Ride Science. "When I was an undergrad at Caltech, I found out about environmental engineering. It's a way for me to work on problems and still be able to pursue my interest in environmental science."

Into the Wild

Today, Ali and her students visit beaches and take water samples so they can measure dangerous microbes from leaked sewage. The goal: to find the sources of pollution to prevent further hazards. "I try to get out into the field and do a lot of water sampling with my students." And even though Ali teaches a lot, she still takes time to ride the waves. Hang ten!

An environmental engineer

An environmental engineer finds ways to protect our natural resources. Ali tries to prevent sewage from ending up in swimming areas. Other **environmental engineers**

* build structures that prevent soil erosion.
* help design buildings that don't hurt their surroundings.
* manage oil spills or toxic waste cleanup.
* predict the effects of building new dams.

Look Around U

What environmental problems do you see in your neighborhood? What do you recommend to improve them?

What Do U Think?

1. The millions of people in New York City get almost all their drinking water from two water tunnels.

   True _____   False _____

2. The Three Gorges Dam in China will be the largest on Earth when it's done.

   True _____   False _____

3. Radioactive waste is safe after ten years.

   True _____   False _____

4. One gallon of spilled oil can ruin 1,000 gallons of drinking water.

   True _____   False _____

Storm Surge

A lot of ocean pollution comes from storm drains—pipes that carry rainwater away. Find the pollutants that sometimes end up in storm drains.

ANTIFREEZE   PAINT

BACTERIA   PESTICIDES

FERTILIZER   SEWAGE

LITTER   SOAP

MOTOR OIL

```
Q  P  J  W  X  M  C  W  Q  S
R  E  Z  I  L  I  T  R  E  F
K  F  C  K  S  O  N  D  Q  N
E  Z  E  E  R  F  I  T  N  A
S  E  S  R  D  C  A  B  H  L
N  G  Z  E  I  H  P  J  H  L
B  A  C  T  E  R  I  A  P  Y
S  W  S  T  Q  Q  A  A  K  V
K  E  L  I  O  R  O  T  O  M
P  S  U  L  C  S  Z  I  B  Q
```

Want to check your answers? Check 'Em Out on page 32.

"Math is an essential part of my toolbox."

Toy-Building Toolbox

As a boy, Chuck loved to draw and paint—first what he saw in the world, then what he saw in his mind. After a degree in sculpture, he wanted to make *movable* sculptures, so he went back to school to study mechanical engineering. "Engineering was the discipline that gave me the tools to build the kind of ideas that I had," he says.

CHUCK HOBERMAN
Hoberman Designs, Hoberman Associates

More than Meets the Eye

Chuck Hoberman likes to make things disappear— almost. You may have played with one of his toy spheres that shrink from the size of a beach ball to the size of an orange. If you watched the 2002 Winter Olympics, you probably saw athletes accept medals under his 22-meter (72-foot) wide arch, which could open up like your eye's iris.

Big (and Little) Dreams

Chuck started two companies to put his designs to work in toys, art, and architecture. He's already filed for 17 patents, so what's next? "I want to see my ideas realized in ways that help people," he tells Sally Ride Science. And his ideas range from machines the size of molecules to retractable stadium rooftops. "The limits are far beyond what I've actually done so far."

Chuck designed the Hoberman Arch for the 2002 Winter Olympics.

An inventor is someone who comes up with new, useful ideas, either from scratch or by combining old ones. Chuck is a sculptor and mechanical engineer who makes unfolding structures. An **inventor** might work in

* a research laboratory.
* a basement workshop.
* a hi-tech company.
* a hospital.

I Like Magic

If you invented something that could shrink to one-tenth its normal size, then expand again, what would you invent?

Mix It Up

Pick one word from each column and combine them. Would that invention be useful? What would it look like? Grab a piece of paper and sketch some ideas. Then repeat—24 more times!

Column 1	Column 2
flying	car
edible	house
waterproof	computer
disposable	jacket
camouflage	toy

Chuck's invention, "Switch Pitch," changes color in midair.

Step by Step

Chuck uses several methods to invent things. He builds models with paper and plastic. He draws sketches. He imagines things in his mind. He programs simulations on computers. Let's say you wanted to build something new. What order might you use these steps in?

1. _____ 2. _____ 3. _____ 4. _____

a) models   b) sketches   c) computer   d) imagine

ANGELA BELCHER
Massachusetts Institute of Technology

Seashore Inspiration

What can an engineer learn from a seashell? In graduate school, Angela Belcher studied the abalone shellfish. "The organism has learned how to make a shell better than we can as materials scientists," she tells Sally Ride Science. Imagine a flawless brick wall so small the bricks are individual molecules, a wall that builds itself and is completely recyclable. Now you get the picture.

A Factory in a Beaker?

What if you could persuade nature to build things in any shape, out of anything, one delicate atom at a time? That's the goal of Angela's lab. The trick is getting tiny biological parts, such as viruses and bacteria, to work with nonbiological parts, such as the atoms used to build computer chips. Eventually, Angela hopes to have perfect tiny computer chip circuitry growing in beakers on her tabletop.

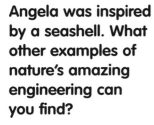

Angela was inspired by a seashell. What other examples of nature's amazing engineering can you find?

Room for Growth

Angela also plans materials that can diagnose cancer, store vaccines, replace bones, and form lighter cars. "A lot of it is unraveling the secrets of nature and then applying what you learn in a way that can benefit society," she says. Next time you're at the beach, take notes. You might unravel a secret or two.

A materials engineer

creates new materials with new features or improves existing ones. Angela uses nature to produce new materials. Other **materials engineers**

* improve sports equipment.
* purify metals removed from mines.
* design fabrics that are waterproof, fireproof, or bulletproof.
* find ways to recycle old materials.

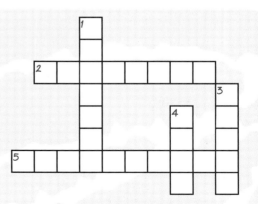

Bees are some of nature's tiniest engineers.

Your Turn

As a materials engineer, if you could invent a new material with any special properties, what would you invent?

_____

_____

It's a Small World

Angela works with nanotechnology, objects no more than 100 nanometers big. A nanometer (nm) is a billionth of a meter! For comparison, match the objects with their measurements

Thickness of a soap bubble	100,000 nm
DNA width	10,000 nm
Blood cell	150 nm
Carbon atom	2 nm
Width of a hair	.07 nm

Materials Matrix

Scientists have found some stupendous materials in nature.

Across
2. These shed water, insulate against cold, and are almost as light as air.
5. This "buggy" thread is stronger than steel for its weight, but stretchy.

Down
1. This is used on drill bits to cut through rock.
3. The pads on this lizard's feet let it climb walls.

4. This covers your whole body and can heal itself.

Want to check your answers? Check 'Em Out on page 32.

Krishna Shenoy
Stanford University

Brainy Scientist

Reading minds sounds like it belongs in science fiction, not in a science lab. But Krishna Shenoy spends lab time reading the minds of monkeys. He's designed a computer system to intercept the signals from neurons, or nerve cells, in the monkey's brain. The signals are directed to a computer so the monkey can move a computer cursor just by thinking about it!

Power of Thought

Krishna's research on how the brain communicates with muscles may lead to the development of new prosthetics, or artificial body parts. He's working on limbs that can be controlled by people's thoughts. "We're developing technology that can help physicians heal people," he tells Sally Ride Science. "I'm proud of that."

Path to the Brain

As an undergrad, Krishna became interested in the brain, then went on to receive a PhD in electrical engineering. It was the perfect marriage. "We didn't know nearly enough about the brain back then, and we didn't have the electronics. We're so far beyond that now." Many people's lives will be touched by today's high-tech tools in the hands of neuroengineers like Krishna.

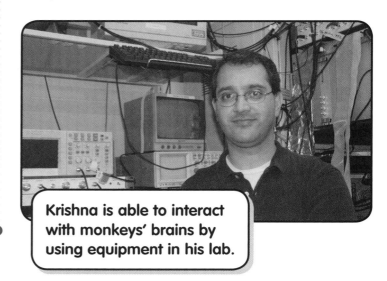

Krishna is able to interact with monkeys' brains by using equipment in his lab.

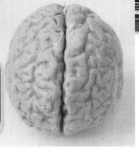

A neuroengineer designs electronic devices that can interact with the brain and nervous system. Krishna studies how the brain communicates with our arms and legs in hopes of designing thought-controlled prosthetics. Other **neuroengineers**

✳ design cochlear implants, tiny devices placed inside the ear that help deaf people hear again.

✳ create pacemakers to help keep hearts beating.

✳ research new devices that work with the nervous system to control pain.

> Your brain has two sides, called hemispheres.

Hot is Cool

Prepare three bowls of water. Fill one with hot water. (Careful! Don't get the water too hot.) Fill another with ice water, and the third with room temperature water.

Put your left hand in the hot bowl and your right hand in the cold bowl. After about 30 seconds, take out both hands and put them in the middle bowl. How does each hand feel? Can you guess why?

Where are the Words?

Unscramble the words and then search for them.

1. There are 100 billion neurons in the _____ that send information all around the body. AINBR

2. Cochlear implants are small electronic devices that help deaf people _____ by transmitting signals to the brain. REAH

3. Scientists have created devices that link brain commands to a _____ on a computer screen. CORRUS

4. In the future, scientists want to be able to help people control mechanical _____ or _____ with only their thoughts! RAMS ELGS

R	O	S	R	U	C
M	H	L	O	N	R
A	E	N	I	L	B
G	A	A	Q	E	D
R	R	E	S	G	A
B	A	R	M	S	N
Z	Q	R	Q	N	P

Want to check your answers? Check 'Em Out on page 32.

"I want to plop a rover on Mars and have it call back when it finds interesting science."

Robot Roommates

Ayanna also finds ways for robots to cooperate with people—in space or on Earth. Astronauts may build Moon colonies alongside bots, but back at home, someone old or sick may need a robot to fetch medicine from another room. "Robots are going to become part of our everyday lives," Ayanna says.

AYANNA HOWARD

NASA Jet Propulsion Laboratory (JPL)

Bio a No-Go

When she was in seventh grade, Ayanna Howard saw a TV show called *The Bionic Woman*. It was about a woman who was rebuilt with robotic limbs after an accident, and it made Ayanna want to study to be a medical doctor. Then she had to dissect a frog and decided she hated biology. From then on, it was all robotics. Now Ayanna finds ways for robots to navigate distant lands on their own.

Thoughts for Bots

The trick is getting robots to think like people. Ayanna programs their artificial intelligence to be flexible so they can react to surprises. They can also learn as they go. But engineering is more than just understanding how humans think. "I come up with a beautiful theory," Ayanna tells Sally Ride Science, "and then I gotta get it working on the rover."

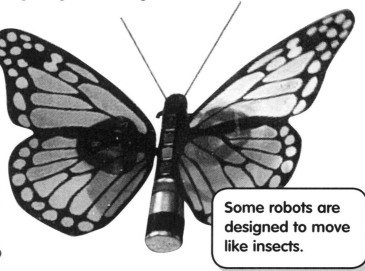

Some robots are designed to move like insects.

A robotics engineer

programs, designs, or builds machines that can do tasks on their own. Ayanna programs robots to explore Mars and to cooperate with people. Other **robotics engineers**

* develop artificial muscles to replace motors and pistons.
* design characters for science fiction movies.
* build robots to do dangerous jobs, such as mining or toxic-waste cleanup.
* invent tiny robots that can move like snakes or bugs.

Your Own Robot

Imagine that you could design your own personal robot. What would you program it to do? What would it look like?

What Do U Think?

1. Robots can run faster than humans.

True _____ False _____

2. Robots are no good at swimming.

True _____ False _____

3. Someone built a robot out of LEGO bricks that can solve a Rubik's Cube.

True _____ False _____

4. Just like R2-D2, robots are better at understanding speech than producing it.

True _____ False _____

Where's WaldoBot?

Find some of the places where robots currently work.

BATTLEFIELDS   HOSPITALS

FACTORIES   MINES

FARMS   NUCLEAR PLANTS

HOLLYWOOD   OCEANS

HOMES   SPACE

```
H O M E S O C W Y P B R R
B A T T L E F I E L D S D
O I H O S P I T A L S R O
G N K V K M Q R V L O B X
S H O L L Y W O O D H V V
X E P I P F F C C T Q E E
S T N A L P R A E L C U N
V M S I U R S P A C E A J
G U B K M W B E N Q Q K F
I Q I R F A R M S W B E C
```

Want to check your answers? Check 'Em Out on page 32.

25

EMIR JOSE MACARI
University of Texas at Brownsville

Not Too Wet, Not Too Dry

Emir Jose Macari loves to go to the beach and to build sand castles—and being a soil engineer comes in handy. "If the soil is too wet, the castle slumps. If it's too dry, it crumbles. A little bit of moisture creates suction and keeps the sand particles together so you can build beautiful sand castles." Don't ever compete against a soil engineer in a sand-castle building contest!

Dirt Detective

Emir studies how different types of soil behave in earthquakes. When he was working on his PhD in 1985, a huge earthquake struck his native Mexico City, demolishing large parts of the city. What made the earthquake so destructive? Emir investigated the soil for answers. It turns out that Mexico City is built on an old lakebed. So when the ground shakes, the waterlogged soil becomes like quicksand, making buildings sink and fall apart. Emir used this knowledge to help engineers design safer buildings. Thanks Emir, for doing such good work in such a "dirty" job.

"Soil is a very interesting material," Emir tells Sally Ride Science. "Everything we build has to be on top of it."

A soil engineer studies the properties of soil and how well different types of soil hold water. Emir uses his knowledge to help design earthquake-proof buildings. **Soil engineers** also

* design plans to clean up soil contaminated by pollution.
* use measurements of soil from the Moon to help design structures that may stand on the Moon one day.
* test soil in an area to help design landfills.
* design levees that can protect us from devastating floods.

Chicken Chuckle

Q. Why did the chicken cross the road, roll in the dirt and cross the road again?

A. Because it was a dirty double-crosser.

Dig It and Build It

Choose two of your Observation Areas from the activity below. Test to see how well a building would stand up on it. Try different weight "buildings," such as a box of oatmeal and a glass filled with marbles. What happens with each?

Can You Dig It?

Check out the soil in different areas of your yard or neighborhood. Dig it, think about it, and log it.

SOIL FEATURE	OBSERVATION AREA #1	OBSERVATION AREA #2	OBSERVATION AREA #3
Texture – Is it sticky, crumbly, smooth, gritty, etc.?			
Size of particles – Small? Medium? Large?			
Compactness - How many inches will a pencil go into the soil?			
Color – Such as brown, red, tan, gray, black, etc.			

MARK DUNZO

Kimley-Horn

Sensing a Problem

When Mark Dunzo gets stuck in traffic, instead of getting frustrated, he thinks about ways to get the cars moving. Mark designs Intelligent Transportation Systems (ITS) that keep track of the flow of cars, and can change the timing of lights. "Sensors can tell if the traffic flow is heavy, like after a ball game," Mark tells Sally Ride Science. "Then the sensors can communicate back to the computer system and say, 'Hey, it's time to use the ball game timing,' and they keep certain lights green longer."

On the Road

As a kid, Mark wanted to be an engineer like his dad. Then in college he realized that instead of building things, what he really loved were cars, buses, trains, and highways—and suddenly he was on the road to a career.

How it Works

The sensors Mark uses consist of loops of wire under the road in front of traffic lights. When a car passes over the wires, it sends a message to a central computer. Thanks to Mark's ITS, the computer can coordinate traffic all around the city.

"Being able to take data and technology and create a system that helps people, that's our art."

A transportation engineer

A transportation engineer works on all areas of transportation, including planning how people and vehicles get around, and designing the buildings for those vehicles. Mark designs smart systems for city traffic lights. Other **transportation engineers**

✷ design city bike paths that are scenic and safe.

✷ design airports, or coordinate the air traffic system.

✷ design freight terminals, where the goods carried by trains are transferred to boats or trucks.

Walk, Don't Walk

When you push the walk button at an intersection, you've probably noticed it doesn't immediately turn the light green. Mark says that's not what it's designed to do. Pushing the button makes one small change. What do you think that is? Observe it next time you cross.

Traffic Tee Hee

Q. What goes through towns, up and over hills, but doesn't move?

A. The road!

Keep 'Em Moving

To limit pollution, traffic lights are designed to prevent too many cars from idling. Check out a traffic light at an intersection near you. What happens on both streets?

Gather data several times, at different times of day.

Name of street	Time of day	Number of cars through the light	Number of cars left behind	Length of time between lights

Your conclusion: What does your neighborhood system need? How would you improve it?

Want to check your answers? Check 'Em Out on page 32.

About Me...

My name is _____ .

I'm in grade _____ at _____ school.

It would be cool to work

❑ In a lab
❑ In space
❑ In a movie studio
(other) _____

❑ In a hospital
❑ In nature
❑ At an amusement park

I like

❑ Building models
❑ Using computers
❑ Sketching my ideas
(other) _____

❑ Doing experiments
❑ Working with friends
❑ Solving math problems

If I could work on a big project, it would be a(n)

❑ Oil-spill cleanup
❑ New highway system
❑ Supercomputer
(other) _____

❑ Mars rover
❑ Artificial leg
❑ Supersonic jet

When something breaks, I

❑ Throw it out
❑ Fix it
❑ Figure out how it works
(other) _____

❑ Think of a better design
❑ Find a new use for it
❑ Take it apart

★ My favorite subjects in school are _____

_____

★ If I could find a solution to a problem, it would be _____

_____

★ If I started a business to sell a new invention, I would sell

_____

★ I think the biggest challenge for engineers today is _____

_____

★ Sometimes I wonder how things work, like _____

_____

★ I like working by myself when _____

_____

★ I prefer ❏ designing things ❏ building things, because

_____

★ Someone who really inspires me or encourages me is

_____ because _____

_____

★ If I could invite an engineer to visit my school, I would invite

_____

I would invite her or him because _____

_____

★ My dream engineering job would be _____

_____

CHECK 'EM OUT: Answers

CHEMICAL ENGINEER, page 9

Chemical Recipes

$C_{12}H_{22}O_{11}$: Sugar
H_2O: Water
NaCl: Salt
CO_2: Carbon Dioxide
$NaHCO_3$: Baking Soda

CIVIL ENGINEER, page 11

Civil Projects

Across
5. Chunnel
7. island
Down
1. skyscraper
2. implode
3. aqueducts
4. kinetic
6. Big Dig

DESIGN ENGINEER, page 15

Feature Finder

ENVIRONMENTAL ENGINEER, page 17

What Do U Think?

1. True. A third will be completed in 2020.
2. True.
3. False. It can still be dangerous after hundreds of years.
4. True. It can ruin a MILLION gallons.

Storm Surge

```
Q P J W X M C W Q S
R E Z I L I T R E F
K F C K S O N D Q N
E Z E E R F I T N A
S E S R D C A B H L
N G Z E I H P J H L
B A C T E R I A P Y
S W S T Q Q A A K V
K E L I O R O T O M
P S U L C S Z I B Q
```

MATERIALS ENGINEER, page 21

It's a Small World

Thickness of a soap bubble: 150 nm
DNA width: 2 nm
Blood cell: 10,000 nm
Carbon atom: .07 nm
Width of a hair: 100,000 nm

Materials Matrix

Across
2. feathers
5. spider silk
Down
1. diamond
3. gecko
4. skin

NEUROENGINEER, page 23

Where are the Words?

brain, hear, cursor, arms, legs

```
R O S R U C
M H L O N R
A E N L B
G A A Q E D
R R E S G
B A R M S N
Z Q R Q N P
```

ROBOTICS ENGINEER, page 25

What Do U Think?

1. False. Running requires a lot balance that robots don't have yet.
2. False. Robotic submarines can go much deeper than humans. Some engineers are also researching ways to make robots swim like fish.
3. True.
4. False.

Where's WaldoBot?

```
H O M E S O C W Y P B R R
B A T T L E F I E L D S D
O I H O S P I T A L S R O
G N K V K M Q R V L O B X
S H O L L Y W O O D H V V
X E P I F F C C T Q E E
S T N A L P R A E L C U N
V M S I U R S P A C E A J
G U B K M W B E N Q Q K F
I Q I R F A R M S W B E C
```

TRANSPORTATION ENGINEER, page 29

Walk, Don't Walk

It's designed to turn green in the usual amount of time, but then it takes more time to go from green to red—long enough for you to cross the street.